M000166239

Turning Tantrums Into Triumphs

Table of Contents

Copyright © 2018 Pamela Li.

Copyright © 2018 Pamela Li.

Turning Tantrums Into Triumphs

By Pamela Li

https://www.parentingforbrain.com/

https://www.facebook.com/parentingforbrain/

Copyright © 2018 Pamela Li.

Copyright © 2018 Pamela Li.

Chapter 1
Introduction

There is never a shortage of parenting advice.

As a young child's mother, I get advice frequently, some unsolicited, from friends, random strangers, parenting experts, TV personalities and of course parenting books.

Most of them preach strategies that can lead to the behavioral changes parents want to see quickly.

But these pieces of advice usually lack scientific evidence on whether they are truly good for children and whether they are healthy long-term solutions.

Parenting is one of the most important and difficult jobs I have ever had.

As a former engineer, I want to know the nuts and bolts of parenting.

I want the answers to all the hows and whys.

I want to know that what I do is truly good for my child and not just more convenient for me.

I want to know that my action will benefit my child not only now, but also in the long run.

This eBook is a result of studying over a thousand clinical studies and discussing with child psychology specialists.

Like everyone else, I have opinions, too. But who cares about that?

What really matters is providing parents with the right scientific information for them to make their own decisions.

I have written this eBook with the busy parents in mind. It is short and concise.

I want to help parents get relevant information quickly and easily.

However, a quick fix is not the goal here because the focus is on the long-term benefits of your child.

Copyright © 2018 Pamela Li.

Parenting is never easy. It requires plenty of patience and self-discipline to produce good results.

Taking shortcuts will only sow the seeds of future trouble and result in a bad relationship with your child.

Keep this in mind whenever you are in doubts. Good things come to those who wait.

In the next chapter, I will first discuss some toddler tantrum basics.

Then, a step-by-step guide to stop toddler tantrums, named CRAFT, will be introduced.

I will also talk about the tantrum dos and don'ts.

At the end, I will share with you my own experience in dealing with my daughter's tantrums.

Throughout the book, I use "he" and "she" alternately. But everything I talk about pertains to children of both genders unless otherwise stated. Details in stories and personal

Copyright © 2018 Pamela Li.

experiences mentioned here may be modified to protect privacy.

Copyright © 2018 Pamela Li.

Chapter 2
Temper Tantrum Basics

What Are Temper Tantrums?

Temper tantrums are intense storms of emotions, which typically include anger, loss, disappointment and deep frustration.

They are disruptive and unpleasant.

In toddlers, these emotional outbreaks can lead to crying, screaming, back-arching, arms flailing, thrashing, falling on the ground, kicking, biting, hitting, throwing things, banging the head or holding breath.

As all parents know, living with a toddler sometimes feels like living with a tantrum landmine. Young children can have tantrums over almost anything.

Mom: Here is your sandwich.

Toddler: NOOOOOO!

Mom: Ok, no sandwich then.

Toddler: NOOOOOO!

Mom: So, what do you want?

Tantrum pursues.

Most temper tantrums are also sudden and fierce.

One minute you and your child are enjoying your meals together.

The next minute she's whimpering because you cut her chicken into pieces, but she wants to cut it by herself.

These behaviors are generally referred to as "temper tantrums".

However, there are two very different types of tantrums — emotional tantrums and Little Nero tantrums.
(Sunderland, 2006)

Temper tantrums are not always about trying to control or manipulate parents.

Copyright © 2018 Pamela Li.

In fact, most tantrums are not manipulative.

They are out-of-control emotions.

Emotional tantrums are common in young toddlers (aged 2-3 years old). Children that young are simply not capable of reasoning or manipulating.

For older children (> 3.5 years old), it is a mixed bag.

Older toddlers are still not experts in the emotion regulating department.

Therefore, they can have emotional tantrums, too.

But depending on parents' reaction to the child's previous tantrums, some children do learn to use tantrums to get what they want.

That is when you have Little Nero tantrums.

But even when children throw Little Nero tantrums, things can get out of hand and Little Nero tantrums turn into emotional tantrums.

Copyright © 2018 Pamela Li.

What Causes Emotional Tantrums?

Temper tantrums are natural reactions to out-of-control emotions.

They are not behavioral problems and they are a normal part of toddlers' development.

Tantrums usually result from unmet needs or desires.

They are more likely to appear in young children because this is when they learn that they are individuals.

They realize they are separate from their parents and they want to seek autonomy. But they lack the way to do so.

If you worry that you are raising a tyrant, take heart – a tantrum throwing toddler is not a spoiled child.

Toddlers' lives may seem cushy. Sure, they have 12 hours of sleep every night, plenty of playing and no working. All their meals are prepared for. Baths are given while they play with rubber ducks.

I'd like that, too. (Ok, may be not the bathing part!)

However, toddlers' lives are not as rosy as they seem.

Here is a typical toddler day.

Toddler: I don't want to eat this.

Dad: No, you have to eat this.

Toddler: I don't want to brush my teeth.

Dad: No, you have to brush your teeth.

Toddler: I don't want to wear socks.

Dad: No, you have to wear socks.

Toddler: I don't want to leave the playground.

Dad: No, you have to leave.

Do they sound like dream lives to you?

Let's think for a moment from the child's perspective.

Babies come to this world with no knowledge of anything. They have zero understanding of how things work.

Imagine if you wake up one day on an alien planet.

You don't speak the aliens' language and you don't understand their logic.

You have to relearn every aspect and every bit of your existence from scratch.

This is probably how young children feel, being on an alien planet learning every new thing and every new rule.

But toddlerhood is an exciting time for them.

Toddlers have just become aware of themselves as individuals separate from their parents.

They are now walking better and discovering the world from a new angle.

They want to explore, go everywhere and touch everything. They want to try new things.

Copyright © 2018 Pamela Li.

So, they look to their parents
for *safety* because exploring something they
have never seen before is scary.

They have just discovered tools, but they
don't have the motor skills fine-tuned enough to
get the results they want.

When they're sad that they cannot lift that
tool, they want *comfort* from their parents. They
want *help* to complete their project.

They are enthusiastic. When they figure
out how to stand up on the high chair, they want
to *share* their joy with their parents.

But instead, all they get is parents yelling
"no", "stop" and "bad" at them for no apparent
reason.

"*What?*"

For two years, despite their best effort in
learning alien rules and practicing alien skills, they
still do not meet their parents' expectation and get
yelled at all day long.

If it were you, wouldn't you be upset, too?

Copyright © 2018 Pamela Li.

When toddlers are upset, they feel strong emotions that they have yet learned to manage.

While babies' stress response systems (e.g. crying) are mature at birth for survival reasons, their emotion regulation systems have not been developed.

In fact, the part of the brain that provides rational control over emotions does not mature until later in life, much later (McGill University, n.d.).

That is why not only toddlers, but also older children and even teenagers can throw massive tantrums when they experience emotion dysregulation.

Adults are not completely immune either.

Imagine how it feels when you are very excited about receiving a new computer. You try to surf the internet but cannot connect to the network no matter how hard you try.

It's very frustrating, right?

Do you swear, pound the keyboard, or slam the door while walking out?

That is the grownup version of a tantrum.

Your fight-or-flight hormone is raging. You can't help it.

Toddlers having emotional tantrums are going through hellish turmoil inside.

To make things worse, the lack of vocabulary to express themselves adds to their anger and frustration.

Temper tantrums then become their outlets and their words.

They are not trying to piss you off.

They are just trying to express their feelings or make their alien world work better in one of the very few ways they know how.

Children are not born defiant. Having an emotional tantrum is not being defiant.

When toddlers have meltdowns,
they are telling us that they are
in deep pain. They cannot cope

Copyright © 2018 Pamela Li.

*on their own. They need our
help, not punishment.*

How Common Are Tantrums?

Toddler tantrums are normal, especially for little kids who are not yet able to verbally express their needs and frustrations.

This developmentally appropriate behavior starts approximately at age two, thereby comes the term "terrible-twos".

Having tantrums is a nearly universal behavior among young children. It is the most common behavioral problem reported by parents to pediatricians.

If a child does not have them during the twos, he or she may have them at three or later.

A study conducted by the University of Wisconsin shows that well over 80% of children start having tantrums at 18-24 months.

At 30-36 months, over 90% have them.

But mercifully, almost half are done by age four (Potegal & Davidson, 2003).

Copyright © 2018 Pamela Li.

Many children have tantrums on an average of once per day.

Most tantrums last between 30 seconds to 1 minute. 75% of them are less than 5 minutes (Potegal, et al., 2003).

So, you are not alone.

Copyright © 2018 Pamela Li.

Copyright © 2018 Pamela Li. 16

Chapter 3
The Science of Temper Tantrums

Bad Tantrums Are Good ... Really

A human brain is made up of millions and millions of brain cells[1].

An adult brain has around 100 billion cells.

Surprisingly, a baby's brain has a lot more brain cells than a grownup's.

But not all of these brain cells and connections will remain as the child grows.[2]

Starting from before birth and during the first year of an infant's life, brain cells develop trillions of connections rapidly among themselves.

---

[1] neurons

[2] synapses

Copyright © 2018 Pamela Li.

Ultimately, this network of connections will determine how a child thinks and acts.

To develop this network, one needs life experiences.

Different life experiences will activate different networks of brain cells.

When cells are activated, their connections are created or strengthened[3].

Eventually, unused cells and connections are eliminated[4] (Huttenlocher, 1984).

This use-it-or-lose-it process is what allows human to survive and adapt to different types of habitats all over the world.

Babies can adapt flexibly to any environment they're born into without the constraint of having too many hardwired connections.

---

[3] myelination

[4] synaptic pruning

Copyright © 2018 Pamela Li.

Because of that, the benefits of creating a brain in this way are enormous.

But so are the costs and risks.

First, children require a lot of care before they can be independent.

Second, experiences during these formative years can have profound impacts on the children's lives (Aamodt & Wang, 2011).

Temper tantrums are some of the most crucial life experiences in sculpting toddler brains.

When having a tantrum, if the child can regulate emotions successfully, proper cell connections associated with the event will form.

Without such experiences, those preexisting connections will be pruned and lost.

Even worse, if the tantrums are handled badly, cell connections associated with the negative experience will be created instead.

Neural circuits are harder to change as a child grows older and they are much harder to change in adulthood.

Toddler tantrums are therefore early life experiences that provide the perfect opportunities for a child to grow a proper, solid neural foundation.

Not only are temper tantrums normal, but they are also desirable in facilitating a child's emotional growth.

Having a tantrum is really not a bad thing.

Why Are Emotional Tantrums So Hard to Stop?

Tantrums are taxing on parents' minds and bodies.

Not only do tantrums happen often, but they are also hard to stop once they start.

Why is that so?

In evolution terms, our brains are composed of three layers.

- *Survival brain*[5] - the bottom or inner most layer regulates automatic bodily functions such as heartbeat and breathing. It mobilizes fight-or-flight[6] behavior in times of threat.

- *Emotional brain*[7] - the middle layer activates positive or negative emotions and evaluates situations very quickly for survival.

- *Thinking brain*[8] - the top layer is the executive of the brain. It performs

---

[5] brain stem (aka reptilian brain)

[6] fight-flight-freeze-faint response

[7] limbic system (aka mammalian brain)

[8] cortex, (aka logical brain)

Copyright © 2018 Pamela Li.

reasoning and manages emotions and

behavior.

So, the thinking brain is critical in inhibiting responses and regulating emotions.

And to do so effectively, extensive connections within and among the different layers of the brain are needed.

There are two major reasons why emotional tantrums are so hard to stop.

First, the thinking brain[9] is needed to intelligently regulate our thoughts, actions and emotions (Arnsten, 2009).

But this part of the brain does not start developing until around age 3.

Almost every parent can attest that you cannot reason with 2-year-olds.

It is not because they are stubborn.

_____

[9] specifically, the prefrontal cortex inside the thinking brain

Copyright © 2018 Pamela Li.

Toddlers simply do not have the capability to do so. That part of the brain is just not there yet.

Once it starts developing, the thinking brain, especially the decision-making part, does not become mature until the child reaches mid-twenties.

Because of this, older children's emotional tantrums can still be hard to stop.

It takes a lot of life experiences to grow and shape a human brain.

The thinking brain has a lot of growing up to do, figuratively and neurologically.

Second, when a toddler is overcome by stress, the emotional brain[10] goes on high alert.

It triggers the release of stress hormones and several other chemicals[11].

---

[10] specifically, amygdala inside the emotional brain

[11] including cortisol, noradrenaline, dopamine, etc.

These chemicals "turn on" the heart and muscles and "turn off" other non-essential functions such as reasoning in the thinking brain for a quick response to distress.

These are good reactions if you are trying to run away from a lion like our ancestors did.

However, during a tantrum, these chemicals also intensify the emotions while impairing the thinking brain.

The thinking brain is essentially "offline" and the emotional brain takes over.

Imagine the emotional brain is the gas pedal in a car while the thinking brain is the brake.

What would happen if you drive a car in which the gas pedal is pressed to the car floor, but the brake is broken?

Such a runaway car will most likely end up crashing.

Toddler tantrums are exactly like that.

They can escalate and become out of control.

Copyright © 2018 Pamela Li.

But remember, the child cannot help it herself because her thinking brain is not present or mature enough.

She needs *your* help.

Turning Tantrums into Triumphs

Emotion regulation is the child's effort to manage, inhibit, enhance or modulate emotions.

It is the key to social competence which affects a child's later functioning across peer and school contexts (Keane & Calkins, 2004) (Lopes, et al., 2003).

Children who can master emotion regulation develop better friendships (Contreras, et al., 2000).

They have fewer behavioral problems (Eisenberg, et al., 2003).

Many studies have also found that emotionally well-regulated children do better in school.

They are more productive in the classroom.

Copyright © 2018 Pamela Li.

They have better academic performance and higher reading and math scores (Graziano, et al., 2007) (Izard, et al., 2001).

When these children grow up, they are likely to become happier and more satisfied in life (Liliana & Nicoleta, 2014).

On the other hand, poor emotion regulation is related to lower social competence, peer acceptance and peer liking (Eisenberg & Fabes, 1992).

In children, difficulties in regulating emotions such as sadness, guilt, shame, anxiety and anger can lead to internalizing disorders (e.g. depression) and externalizing behaviors (e.g. aggression, violence) (Caspi, et al., 2008).

Hence, the capacity for emotion regulation forms the foundation of a person's future health and success.

Helping children regulate their emotions and arousal is, therefore, one of the parent's most important job.

As we interact with our children, we teach, reinforce and demonstrate emotion regulation.

How we respond during meltdowns lay the groundwork for our kids to learn to handle difficulties in life (Mikulincer, et al., 2003).

We can transform these unpleasant moments into invaluable life lessons and brain network sculpting opportunities.

We can raise children whose thinking brain can prevail over the emotional one.

We can turn tantrums into triumphs.

Copyright © 2018 Pamela Li.

Copyright © 2018 Pamela Li.

Chapter 4
Dealing with Tantrums

Using my own experience, I have created the **CRAFT** method to deal with my child's emotional tantrums.

CRAFT stands for
<u>C</u>alm, <u>R</u>edirect, <u>A</u>cknowledge,
<u>F</u>acilitate, <u>T</u>each.

<u>C</u>RAFT: Calm

Next time when you are faced with your toddler's meltdown, first and foremost, stay calm.

Take a deep breath and don't get angry.

I know it's easier said than done. A tantrum is not a pretty sight. When your child is kicking, screaming, throwing things and making a scene, it is very hard to stay calm.

But it helps to remember that your child is not doing this *to* you.

Copyright © 2018 Pamela Li.

She is not trying to get back at you.

Your child is doing this because she has no control over her emotions yet and she does not cause this.

Remember, tantrums are normal and essential to a child's development.

Every time your child throws a tantrum, her brain grows!

It is not your fault that she is having a tantrum. You are not a bad parent.

It is not your child's fault that she cannot control her emotions yet. She is not a bad child.

Your child is doing what she needs to grow up.

She needs that life experience.

It is crucial for mom and dad to stay calm during a tantrum episode because children mimic what adults do.

That includes having control over emotions.

If you get angry and yell at her when she throws a tantrum, you are demonstrating how she should react when things don't go her way.

But if you keep your cool, you are then teaching her how to face adverse situations gracefully without losing control (Morris, et al., 2007).

Grownups can be overcome by emotions, too.

Stress can shut down your thinking brain in the same way it shuts down your child's.

But you have more awareness to proactively prevent this from happening.

Consciously keep yourself calm. Don't lose your temper.

You can then think clearly to come up with an effective response to the situation.

If it ever comes to a point where you are about to "flip" or "snap", give yourself a time-out (you, not your child).

Leave the room, take a deep breath or take a walk until you can compose yourself.

Tell your child why you must take a break before leaving so that you are not abandoning her.

"Daddy needs to step outside to cool down. I will be back soon."

You are modeling how to regulate your own emotions.

Another reason for staying calm is that emotions, especially negative ones, are contagious (Waters, et al., 2014).

Being angry or negative will also raise your child's stress level and make the situation worse.

Stay positive so that your kid will not feed off negativity.

Research shows that when parents get angry during tantrums, the problems are more likely to continue over time.

But if parents are supportive and set clear limits, fewer behavioral problems appear (Denham, et al., 2000).

If the child is raging and acting violently, contain that behavior first.

Your child must not hit anyone, scream nonstop or break things.

Even if the child is not physically endangering others, overwhelming rage terrifies the child, too. Stop the violent act to protect the child and others around.

If verbal instructions fail, your child is likely too flooded with emotions to listen.

Step in and gently remove or restraint her while explaining what you are doing.

"You are hurting others and I cannot allow that. Let's cool off outside."

"I need to remove you because you hit Uncle Ray. I must keep both of you safe."

CRAFT: Redirect Attention

Sometimes when you sense that a tantrum is coming on, you can diffuse it by promptly addressing the issue at hand or by redirecting the child's attention.

For example, if your child does not want to have his dinner, instead of forcing him to eat which will bring on more emotions, ask him to choose between meat and vegetable.

Asking questions instead of giving commands can redirect the child's focus.

Questions with two simple choices can engage his critical thinking and activate the thinking brain to stay in control.

Exciting the thinking brain by using distractions, such as another toy, a funny face or a silly song.

Use something the child hasn't noticed before or something he will find interesting.

Novel distractions pique a child's curiosity triggering the release of a feel-good chemical[12].

This chemical can reduce stress, raise the child's focus on the new event (Sulzer & Galli, 2003) and take his attention away from the tantrum.

---

[12] dopamine

Copyright © 2018 Pamela Li.

Do it before emotions escalate into a full-fledged tantrum.

Stamp out tantrums before they even start.

CRAFT: Acknowledge

Sometimes, distractions don't work, or they are used too late.

Then, the emotional storm starts, and your child will be in great distress.

The best way to help a child in distress, whether it is caused by anger, frustration or fear, is to acknowledge her feelings and offer her emotional support.

By attending to her emotions, you are directly communicating with her emotional brain which at that moment is in the driver's seat. When you get her attention and the emotional intensity has subsided, you can then talk more to activate her thinking brain and help her reconnect the two brains (Bath, 2006).

Copyright © 2018 Pamela Li.

To begin, simply narrate what is going on in a supportive tone.

"You are very upset because she took your toy."

"You must be very angry because Mommy didn't let you have snack before dinner."

In most cases, acknowledgements like these can instantly turn a toddler's screaming into a quiet sob and some big nods.

You can see the expression "Yes! That's it!" in her eyes.

There are a few things parents must NOT do:

- Reason with the child

- Trivialize her feelings

- Make light of the issue

- Make fun of the child

- Try to stop the crying

- Use a harsh tone

Don't try to reason

When a child's tantrum is in full swing, her system is overloaded with emotions.

The more mature, over-aroused emotional brain has "hijacked" the thinking brain.

The child's rational thinking and verbal communications cannot be accessed.

The child can neither think logically, nor put her feelings into words.

The toddler is experiencing a "brain freeze".

Trying to reason with your toddler or asking her about her feelings at this stage is a waste of time.

You may end up upsetting her and arousing her emotions even more.

Brain research shows that we cannot "teach lessons" to a toddler when she is emotionally aroused; de-escalation and activation of the thinking brain is the primary goal.

Copyright © 2018 Pamela Li.

We can only use reasoning when her thinking brain resumes control.

You may have encountered similar situations with adults.

Sometimes even grownups say or do irrational things when they are outraged.

Afterwards, they say, "I was angry. I don't know what I was thinking."

Well, in those moments, they really were not thinking because they were having a brain freeze like a toddler in tantrums.

Don't trivialize feelings or discount the issue

It is tempting for parents to downplay the situation during a tantrum.

After all, grownups don't usually find balloons flying away a stressful event.

Many parents also mistakenly believe that ignoring negative emotion will make it go away.

But scientists have found that such strategies have the exact opposite effect.

Children whose parents minimize or dismiss their negative feelings tend to have more difficulties regulating emotions. These children have poorer empathic skills, worse social competence and more behavioral problems (Eisenberg, et al., 1996) (Jones, et al., 2002) (Lunkenheimer, et al., 2007).

These negative effects can eventually lead to future mental health issues such as depression and anxiety (Luebbe, et al., 2011).

Don't try to stop the crying

Parents may find it difficult to allow their kids to cry freely as most of us were not allowed to do so when we were kids.

Some of us were stopped kindly ("It's ok. Don't cry.")

Others were distracted, punished, ignored or yelled at ("If you don't stop crying right now, I'll give you something to cry about.")

Sometimes we were praised as "brave" for not crying.

Copyright © 2018 Pamela Li.

We were constantly given the message that crying was bad and unacceptable.

Over the years, we have learned to suppress our own tears making it hard for us to empathize with a crying child.

As a result, many parents have a strong urge to stop their children from crying.

A child crying can also bring out various emotions in the parent.

Some parents feel that crying is a sign of weakness, especially in boys.

They are afraid crying or showing hurtful emotions means the child is weak or less masculine.

They feel *shameful* for their child's behavior.

Some feel that a crying child is a stubborn child being difficult or refusing to let go.

They are *angry* at the child's defiance.

Others see crying as the cause of painful feelings.

They believe as soon as the child stops crying, he will be fine.

They feel *helpless* if they cannot stop the crying and make the child feel better.

Some parents also fear that a child's tears are indication of incompetent parents.

They *lose confidence* or feel *embarrassed* when it happens in public.

Scientifically, there is contradictory evidence on the causes and benefits of crying.

Some researchers find that crying facilitates recovery by releasing pent-up emotions and removing toxic chemicals through tears. But others find that crying sustains negative arousal and makes people feel worse (Hendriks, et al., 2008).

While the exact role of crying is still under debate, the benefit in the form of social support from others is unquestionable (Thoits, 1995).

Even if crying itself does not lead to emotional relief, the understanding, the

Copyright © 2018 Pamela Li.

acceptance and the emotional support from others do.

Crying is a natural reaction to sadness, frustration or pain.

Dealing with big feelings is already hard enough for your child.

Telling him that his feelings are wrong ("It's no big deal"), disapproving his attempt to heal hurts ("Don't cry") or scolding him for something he cannot help ("Stop being a baby") will not make him feel better.

Don't be harsh

Some misinformed but well-intentioned parents believe in giving their children "tough love".

They believe doing so will make their children grow up with the ability to withstand rough situations in life.

But research shows otherwise.

A study was performed in Israel where 18-year-old men must serve in mandatory military service. It was found that male adolescents who grew up in a non-nurturing environment coped and adapted worse in the tough military scenery than those who grew up in a nurturing household (Mayseless, et al., 2003).

Unresponsive and non-nurturing parenting styles are also linked to many behavioral and psychological problems in children (Baumrind, 1967).

It is so important that during tantrums, parents are attuned to their children's emotions, accept their feelings without judgment and be supportive.

Sometimes, a positive acknowledgement alone such as "I know", "You must feel very upset" or "I'm so sorry that you're hurt" is good enough to let a child feel safe and understood.

What parents say matters a lot.

Our words can heal or hurt, not only in the moment but also in the future.

Children internalize parents' words and use them in their private speech. If parents are sympathetic and supportive, children can use those conversations to self-regulate. (WINSLER, et al., 2003).

Conversely, if parents are unsympathetic and judgmental, these conversations become self-criticisms.

The way we talk to our children becomes their inner voice.

CRAFT: Facilitate Emotion Regulation

When a child is overwhelmed by distress, his emotional brain will trigger the release of a stress hormone called cortisol.

Cortisol affects multiple cognitive domains in the brain including perception, attention, memory, and emotional processing.

Although the emotional brain can trigger the hormonal release, it has no mechanism to turn it off. Only the thinking brain can do that. However, the thinking brain is offline under cortisol's influence. The toddler is then stuck in a state of agitation, rage and emotional pain (Stien & Kendall, 2014).

One of the fastest ways to return to hormonal balance is to activate the release of another hormone called oxytocin. Parents can facilitate the release of oxytocin through gentle physical contact such as holding or hugging. This feel-good chemical causes the level of cortisol to plummet so that the thinking brain can resume its normal functioning (Heinrichsa, et al., 2003).

Studies show that children who are cuddled during tantrums have tantrums that are significantly shorter and less frequent (Potegal, et al., 2003).

Before hugging or holding a distressed child, make sure you are calm yourself and you are genuinely supportive.

Otherwise, hugging may cause the child to become even more distressed.

Hugging is not the only way to restore a child's emotional balance.

Some children do not like being touched.

In this case, you can sit next to him and tell him calmly that you are here for him.

Emotional support is an important aspect of social support. It can facilitate a child's emotional regulation (Uchino, et al., 1996).

Some parents worry that hugging or paying attention to a child in tantrums amounts to rewarding his bad behavior.

This may be the case if cuddling is not a common activity or the child is often neglected in daily life.

But for most loving parents who regularly pay attention and cuddle with their child, hugging during meltdowns will only help restore the child's emotional balance.

You are not rewarding undesired behavior.

Remember the runaway car analogy?

If a child is stuck in a runaway car, the parent will try to rescue the child even though the child has gotten into this trouble because he has defied his parents.

Copyright © 2018 Pamela Li.

The parent will not ignore him fearing that will reward the bad behavior.

At that moment, saving the child is obviously more important than worrying about bad behavior being encouraged.

Similarly, if a child is stuck with runaway emotions, the parent should rescue the child first by helping him regulate.

It is much more important to prevent an emotional crash.

Frequent emotional crashes will have many negative long-term health impacts (Bugental, et al., 2003).

Save the child first. You can always lecture later.

CRAFT: Teach

Teach words

After the dust has settled and your child has thoroughly de-escalated from the intense emotional state, hold her close and review what happened.

This is another important moment to turn an unhappy incidence into a big parenting triumph.

Use this opportunity to teach her what to say next time to prevent frustration.

Toddlers with better language skills are less angry and have less tantrums over time (Roben, et al., 2013).

"Instead of throwing a tantrum, you can say "Can you please bring me the cup?"".

"You can just say, "I am upset." or "I don't like this."".

Help your child put feelings into words.

Teach her vocabulary to express herself rather than acting out.

Help her practice saying them.

When parents strive to accept and listen to their children's strong feelings, children will know that they can always come to their parents with problems.

Copyright © 2018 Pamela Li.

They will trust that no matter how angry, frustrated, frightened or sad they feel, they are still loved.

Teach critical thinking and problem solving

Start teaching her critical thinking. Help her develop this important skill.

Tell her why throwing tantrums is not good.

"Because when you scream, I cannot hear you clearly. I don't know what you want. But if you calmly tell me, I can hear you and help you figure out what to do."

Ask her how she can solve the problem differently next time.

"Can you come up with a way to get my attention next time without screaming?"

Critical thinking is a multi-dimensional skill that applies to every part of life. We want our children to develop effective skills in problem solving, constructive conflict resolution, sound decision making and insightful invention. Being

Copyright © 2018 Pamela Li.

able to think critically is a strong predictor of academic and professional success later in life (Gadzella, et al., 1997) (Williams, et al., 2003) (Holmgren & Covin, 1984).

Critical thinking is also a crucial skill for children to proceed into adolescence and later adulthood. It is best learned through discussion with others rather than thinking by oneself (Gokhale, 1995).

Involving your child in this discussion makes her more likely to remember the solution she helps create next time and do that instead of throwing a tantrum (Farrant & Reese, 2000).

Teach narration to enhance brain integration

Narrate the experience.

"Remember how it happened?"

"Yes, that's right. You enjoyed the candy and you wanted another one. But you couldn't reach it because Mommy had put it away. Now you know how to ask, right? Let's practice."

Through parent-guided narration, children learn the forms and functions of talking and how to think about upsetting events.

They also learn to organize their thoughts and understand what has happened.

Being able to talk about an experience afterwards, even a negative one such as a tantrum, has far-reaching benefits.

It creates neural connections for the child to manage future emotional situations.

Making sense is also a significant part of growing a healthy young mind.

Children whose parents narrate past events collaboratively have better memory, more advanced socio-emotional development and higher child well-being (Fivush, et al., 2009) (Marin, et al., 2008).

Teach empathy

Tell her how you feel when she has an outburst.

Teach her about other people's emotions.

"You know when you were upset, Mommy was frustrated, too, because I didn't know what you wanted."

It says to the child that it is alright to have feelings.

Feelings can be controlled and should not be feared.

Explain how her actions can affect others -- an important understanding that forms the basis for empathy.

"Can you give Mommy a kiss to make her feel better, too?"

Teach ourselves

Finally, this is a lesson that is as valuable to the parent as it is to the child.

Through my own experience, I have learned to empathize with my child. While a tantrum is frustrating for adults, it is emotionally painful for the child.

Sometimes, seemingly minor decisions of mine can have powerful impact on her. I come to consciously respect her needs and emotions.

Copyright © 2018 Pamela Li.

Using Punishment

For some parents, punishment is the go-to method to stop tantrums.

But punishment is counter-productive because it does not help restore emotional balance in the child.

Let's say you are suffering from intense physical pain.

The pain is so acute that you drop to the ground and writhe.

Now, if your loved ones punish you, walk away from you or lock you in a room by yourself, wouldn't you get even more upset and feel more hurt?

Harsh responses from parents and punishment for having a tantrum can escalate a child's emotions further.

Instead of reconnecting with his logical thinking, the child becomes more stressed and flooded with emotions.

A child does not learn to self-regulate this way. If a child cannot regulate himself, he will find it difficult to behave in a socially competent manner (Fabes, et al., 2001).

When faced with frustrations later in life, he will struggle to be assertive or have angry outbursts.

When tantrums are met with negative reactions or lack of response, some toddlers may stop crying and appear normal again.

That does not necessarily mean they are not in distress any more.

Emotion suppression is not emotion regulation.

Suppressed feelings are merely swept under the rug.

Sooner or later, those suppressed emotions will catch up with them.

Studies have shown that distressed young children can appear to be calm but still have high stress hormonal levels inside. In some cases, this dissociation between behavioral and physiological reactions can lead to mental health problems later in life (Dutra, et al., 2009).

Punishment, such as time-out or isolation, also cannot help a child calm down.

It only teaches your child that he cannot rely on you to help him when he is in distress. It also tells him that he cannot trust you to understand his grief when he's in pain.

If a child learns early on that expressing big feelings will result in parental anger or punishment, he tends to become either submissive or defiant (Fabes, et al., 2001).

Either way, the child will not have the opportunities to learn to regulate his strong emotions appropriately to develop proper regulation skills.

For many parents, punishment is appealing because it gives the illusion of prompt success in controlling tantrums.

Such belief is very understandable.

When we come home after a long day at work, we are exhausted. We just cannot deal with yet another tantrum. We lose our temper. Our emotional brains have taken over. We punish the child to bring on prompt relief.

We've all been there.

But let's stop for a moment and consider this.

What are our parenting goals?

On one hand, using punishment can stop tantrums quickly and bring on fast relief to the parents. But it is at the expense of the child not being able to learn self-regulation.

On the other hand, using nurturing responses to handle tantrums can be exhausting, at least at the beginning. But your child will benefit from learning emotional regulation for life. And as you help your child learn and grow, you build a close relationship based on trust.

So, during tantrums, is the goal to stop the crying as quickly as possible?

Or is it to help the child gain valuable skills for life and have a good relationship with the parents?

Copyright © 2018 Pamela Li.

The choice is obvious if parents can keep their parenting goals in mind.

A research shows that intentions can alter parents' affective states. Parents who focus on stopping the tantrums have more negative feelings and less sympathy for their children. But parents who focus on creating long lasting relationships and on helping their children cope feel less negative and are more empathetic (Hastings & Grusec, 1998).

If the parents choose to put the child's needs first during tantrums, parents will benefit eventually.

It is not a zero-sum game. It is a tradeoff between short-term relief and long-term happiness.

Another topic of broad interest to parents, caretakers, educators and children's rights activists is using spanking as a form of punishment.

It is one of the last holdouts of old-fashioned childrearing that is still regularly practiced by many parents.

In the latest research at The University of Texas at Austin, Gershoff conducted a new meta-analysis reviewing 50 years of research on spanking. This most complete analysis to date involving over 160,000 children focused only on spanking, which most American believed to be a normal form of discipline, not on potentially abusive behaviors (Gershoff, Jun 2016).

Despite only results on spanking (defined as an open-handed hit on the behind or extremities) were included, the detrimental outcomes were found to be analogous to those of physical abuse, in the same direction and nearly the same strength[13].

Unfortunately, in the face of mounting evidence, many parents are still skeptical and insist spanking is not harmful.

---

[13] Negative outcomes of physical abuse and spanking include decreased moral internalization, increased child aggression, increased child delinquent and antisocial behavior, decreased quality of child-parent relationship, decreased child mental health, increased risk of being a victim of physical abuse, increased adult aggression, increased adult criminal and antisocial behavior, decreased adult mental health, and increased risk of abusing own child or spouse (Gershoff, 2002).

Copyright © 2018 Pamela Li.

To fully understand the negative results, we should look at the physiological impact of being spanked.

Like tantrums, being spanked is a stressful event which causes the child's emotional brain to release stress hormones and chemicals.

If the child has been throwing a tantrum, spanking will then add even more stress hormones to the already high level of hormones in the tiny body.

Excessive exposure to cortisol has multiple health ramifications.

In primate studies, extended exposure of cortisol causes the degeneration of brain cells (Sapolsky, et al., 1990).

In human studies, brain cell atrophy is linked to high levels of cortisol (Carrion, et al., 2007) and spanking.

In brain scan studies, people who have received harsh corporal punishment in childhood are found to have up to 19% smaller brain sizes (Tomoda, et al., 2009). Brain size shrinkage is most prominent in the parts of the brain[14] responsible for memory and learning (Bremner, 1999).

If a child frequently experiences high levels of cortisol (think how often a toddler throws tantrums), his baseline level of stress hormone will become higher than normal (Bugental, et al., 2003).

Chronic elevated levels of stress hormone will likely result in various physical and mental health conditions later in life, such as suppressed immune system, hypertension, depression and anxiety disorders just to name a few (Seaward, 2011).

Having a higher baseline of cortisol also means that the child will be more reactive to any situation and get upset more easily over seemingly little things. Once he is aroused, it is also harder for him to restore balance.

Harmful effects of corporal punishment are real and well documented, even though some

---

[14] hippocampus

parents do not experience those negative outcomes themselves.

But there are also many smokers who do not develop lung cancers. The damages of smoking are still real and scientifically proven.

That is why we shouldn't use anecdotal stories to justify spanking, for the same reason why we don't justify smoking.

Now, all scientific evidence aside, if your boss hits you when you do something he or she does not approve of, will you still respect that person?

Do you want your child to respect you?

Spanking is one of the fastest ways you can lose your child's respect.

He may fear you, but he will not respect you.

Don't confuse fear with respect.

For parents who want to give their children the best, it is not necessary to spank given that there are many other non-violent disciplinary measures. And they are often more effective (Gershoff, 2002).

If you have tried everything mentioned in this book and are still stuck with massive tantrums, you may try "time-out from reinforcement" as a last resort, but only as a last resort.

Only give the child a time-out if

- You have *consistently* tried the **CRAFT** strategy for months,

- Your child physically hurt others or break things, or

- He is too overwhelmed with emotions and you cannot do anything to help him settle down (including hugging him calmly for a long time).

The purpose of time-out is to give the child space away from any stimulations to reduce emotional arousal.

It is a behavioral modification strategy and it should not be used as a punishment.

Do not make it punitive by adding harsh conditions such as confinement, extended isolation, restricted movement or being berated by parents before / afterwards.

Give him the choices before carrying out the time-out.

"You can choose to calm down now, or you can choose to have a time-out to settle down. You have the power to decide this. Which one do you want?"

By allowing the child to make a conscious decision, you are teaching him how to make sound judgement.

When placing your child in a time-out, explain the goal and reassure they are not being abandoned or punished.

"You're going to have a time-out to settle down. I will be right over there. You are not being abandoned or punished. But you need to calm down."

Copyright © 2018 Pamela Li.

If your child refuses to stay in the spot, gently and firmly place him back.

Be kind and firm.

You can mean business without being mean.

Little Nero Tantrums

There are times when a toddler is truly behaving like a Little Nero [15]. He wants something and won't stop screaming and kicking until he gets it.

When a child is in this power-struggle mode, his system is not swamped with hormones or intense emotions.

You can tell by the lack of painful expressions on his face.

---

[15] Nero was the last emperor of the Roman Empire. He was described as spoiled, angry and unhappy.

Despite the lack of emotional overflow, you can still use **CRAFT** to handle such tantrums, but with some cautions.

With this type of tantrums, most parents know they cannot give in or they would be teaching their children to use tantrums to get what they want.

But knowing the theory is different from practicing it.

Children can often be very persistent. I have seen parents who know they should not give in but still do so after several rounds of pleading and tantrums.

These parents think that they are just making an exception.

"Just this *one* time."

But to the kids, those are the results of their actions.

If you are not consistent in keeping limits, your child will be consistently trying to wear you out to get what he wants.

Copyright © 2018 Pamela Li.

Consistency is also necessary among you, your partner and other caretakers.

Research have shown that inconsistent discipline is linked to early behavioral problems and mental health issues in children (Feehan, et al., 1991) .

If your child screams constantly, hits others or breaks properties, gently remove him.

Let him know that you will stay with him, but you will not interact further until he is calm.

If you are in public – a common breeding ground for tantrums – be prepared to leave with your child even if you are in the middle of a gathering, movie or dinner.

Consistency is the key.

No exceptions.

Some parents advocate ignoring the child during Little Nero tantrums.

It may work in some situations where the child intentionally throws a tantrum but remains in good control of his emotions.

In those cases, paying no attention to the child *may* extinguish the bad behavior.

But the ignoring approach should not be used as a rule for every tantrum.

Before ignoring, first make sure the child is not so overpowered by strong emotions that he is not equipped to cope by himself.

The child also must not be hurting anything or anyone, including himself.

Discreetly monitor the child's emotions even when you are "ignoring" him.

A pretend tantrum, if left undealt with for too long, can escalate into a genuine case of uncontrollable emotional storm.

I generally do not recommend ignoring the child or giving him isolated time-outs, unless these are absolute last resorts because these treatments amount to abandonment and rejection.

Through studying the brain scans of toddlers, researchers have found that rejection can have similar effects on the brains as physical pain (Eisenberger, 2012).

Copyright © 2018 Pamela Li.

Inflicting pain on a toddler in tantrum, even though it is only mentally, is like adding fuel to the fire.

It can push the child right over the edge turning a Little Nero tantrum into an emotional one.

Ignoring may teach a child that his behavior is unacceptable, but it does not tell him why the behavior is bad. It also does not teach the proper behavior.

Why not turn this into another brain sculpting moment instead?

Change it into a constructive experience and create productive neural connections.

Since the child can think rationally during a Little Nero tantrum, engage his logical reasoning and teach him something.

As with emotional tantrums, first help the child calm down and get his attention. Acknowledging his desire and mirroring his emotions may be all it takes for him to cool off and be receptive (Karp, 2008).

Copyright © 2018 Pamela Li.

Here is an example on acknowledging and mirroring.

Your child is shouting, "I want this!" with agitation.

Mimic his agitated expression and mildly shout back, "I know you really want this. You really, REALLY want this, right?"

You are mirroring his emotion to let him know that you understand how he feels.

Affirming his needs and attuning to his feelings tells him that you get it.

You get how upset he is and you care about him.

When your child feels validated, you will have his attention and the rational thinking that comes with it.

Half of the battle is won.

Then explain calmly the reason why he cannot have what he wants.

Copyright © 2018 Pamela Li.

"But I'm sorry. You cannot have ice cream before dinner because that would spoil your appetite."

Some children will throw another tantrum on hearing that, but it will be less intense and easier to handle this round by repeating **CRAFT** again.

To summarize, remember
CRAFT.
Calm. Redirect. Acknowledge.
Facilitate. Teach.

Copyright © 2018 Pamela Li.

Chapter 5
Tantrum Do and Don't

Do Prevent

Do you sometimes wonder why your toddler throws a tantrum for no apparent reason?

It could be due to the hidden reasons, **HALT**:

H – Hunger
A – Anger
L – Loneliness
T – Tiredness

Children are more prone to throw fits when they are hungry or tired.

When these physical factors are present, children have lower tolerance for frustration. All it takes is a trigger to set things in motion.

So, set a schedule of sleep-eat-rest to avoid these tantrum traps.

Copyright © 2018 Pamela Li.

And when it does happen, skip attending to the tantrum. Immediately feed him, put him to bed or take care of other physical needs.

Being bored or angry are also common triggers.

If you can avoid stressing your toddler without compromising your limits, it is always worth doing so.

It's much easier to access their logical thinking to prevent a tantrum than to put it out once it starts.

This does not mean you should be permissive and give your child everything he demands.

It only means that whenever possible, do not create a situation where you know your child will be upset.

For example, if you know he is getting bored, give him a busy bag.

Or assign him a task.

"Could you please put those dirty clothes into the laundry basket for me?"

"Can you help me count the number of beans I'm about to cook?"

If you must forbid something your child enjoys, do it as tactfully as you can.

If he must do something he does not like, try to make it fun, make it easier for him to accept and give advance warnings.

Use distractions in advance if you know he will be upset when he cannot have the same toy as his brother's.

Another key to prevent tantrums is to be flexible.

Oftentimes, parents have preconceived notions of things. But not everything has to be done exactly the way you believe they should be.

Perhaps it is ok to go out wearing mismatched socks.

Perhaps it is alright to use the wrong fork for salad.

No harm will be done, right?

Copyright © 2018 Pamela Li.

Parents can eliminate many struggles and tantrums simply by being flexible and open-minded.

Choose your battles.

Reflect on how often you are saying "no".

If you find yourself saying "no" all the time, it is time to review if there are too many rigid rules in your household.

Are they all necessary?

Distinguish between musts and wants.

Toddlers have so little control over what happens to them (alien planet, remember?) It is only reasonable for them to feel frustrated over these seemingly arbitrary rules.

Finally, stress within the family can also affect toddlers even though they may seem too young to understand. Marital tensions, extremely busy schedules, overstressed parents, or upheaval in the family can also provoke tantrums.

Don't Give Up

Strategies introduced in this book most likely will not vanquish toddler tantrums on the spot or the first try.

Remember how we learned to write in school?

Repetitions! (Ervin-Tripp, 2014)

We learn by repeating and practicing the same act over and over. And toddler brains require many, MANY repetitions to learn[16].

Parents need to consistently and persistently implement these strategies to see positive results.

Be patient.

Your toddler will get it eventually. And the wait is worth it.

---

[16] Some argue that physical punishment helps children "learn" faster. But abused children do not "learn". They fear. Fear goes through a separate brain circuit different from learning, and it damages children's mental health.

Copyright © 2018 Pamela Li.

But of course, no parenting advice can work for every child.

What I present here are evidence-based strategies that are more likely to produce positive long-term results, but they may not fit every child.

Parents should adapt them to different needs of their kid.

These strategies also only address the child's needs but not the parent's wish to stop tantrums immediately.

Ultimately, parents need to make the decisions to create a balance between the child's needs and their own sanity.

Don't get stressed out if you cannot do every step every single time.

No one can.

I certainly cannot.

You will probably find me yelling at my kid too if I've been driven up the wall.

It's OK to slip once in a while.

Unless it is a traumatic event, a one-off incident is not going to scar your child for life.

It is the repeated experience and the prevailing atmosphere at home that will affect the outcomes.

Strive to create a happy home with positive attitudes, even when facing difficult moments.

If you can focus on using those situations as teaching moments, you will have a more positive mindset and most likely more positive outcomes.

Copyright © 2018 Pamela Li.

Chapter 6
Is My Child Born Defiant?

Some parents wonder if their children are just born difficult and defiant. They doubt the advice in this book will work for those "bad seeds".

Nature versus nurture is a centuries-old debate.

People are often worked up over this debate because many of us have learned in high school about the deterministic properties of some genetic traits, such as the color of the eyes, the type of hair, etc.

You can either have blue eyes or green eyes, straight hair or curly hair, one or the other.

Characteristics like these are encoded in our gene. They do not change with the environment.

But personality traits work in a different manner.

Copyright © 2018 Pamela Li.

Although some characteristics of a child's personality, like temperament, are largely determined by genetics, life experience can alter how some of the genes are expressed[17] resulting in a different personality.

Life experience can also reshape the brain's neural network by creating and strengthening new neural bonds changing how the child thinks and acts.

Meanwhile, temperament can reciprocally influence the type of life experience a child encounters.

So, nature and nurture interact and affect each other.

Together, they shape the child's personality and behavior. It is not one or the other.

This explains why no parenting strategy is guaranteed to work for every child as the

---

[17] epigenetic modification

Copyright © 2018 Pamela Li.

interaction between parenting practice and genetic heredity is not entirely deterministic.

A team of researchers at the VU University of Amsterdam and the Queensland Brain Institute reviewed 2748 studies involving over 14.5 million pairs of twins. They found that roughly half (49%) of the variations in human traits and diseases are due to genetics, and the other half (51%) to environment (Polderman, et al., 2015).

It is possible that your child has a temperament that falls into the "difficult" category.

But do not despair.

Because there is good news for you.

Turns out difficult temperaments are disproportionately affected by parenting.

Difficult children react more to the quality of parenting than easy children do, for better and for worse.

When raised with good parenting, a difficult child tends to do better in cognitive,

Copyright © 2018 Pamela Li.

academic and social adjustment than their easy counterparts (Pluess, 2010).

Therefore, you should be *thrilled* if you have a difficult child.

Your difficult child has a better chance to succeed, if you do your part in providing good parenting.

For difficult children, simple choices and distractions may not be enough to activate their logical brains.

If that is the case, you need to do more work to restore your child's emotional balance.

Be more patient when helping him restore his emotional balance. Spend more time teaching him to express his feelings with words.

With enough patience and persistence, and some trial and error, even a difficult child can learn how to integrate their logical and emotional brains and stop using tantrums as outlets (Bakermans-Kranenburg & Ijzendoorn, 2011).

Copyright © 2018 Pamela Li.

It may take a long time to get through to your child and the process may be painstaking, but the reward is tremendous.

Copyright © 2018 Pamela Li.

Copyright © 2018 Pamela Li.

Chapter 7

Is Terrible Twos "Just A Phase"?

Most parents and pediatricians alike believe that terrible-twos is simply a phase that will eventually pass.

Although the tantrum stage is temporary, the impacts on the child are long lasting (Shonkoff, n.d.).

Emotional regulation is a crucial skill in life. It forms the basis of all future learning and behavior (Thompson, 1991).

A child lacking emotion regulation skills tends to have worse attention and problem-solving capabilities. She tends to perform worse in school (Raver, 2003).

Not being able to self-control causes the child to have worse social competence (Petrides, 2006).

As a result, the child will be at higher risk for negative outcomes such as school dropout,

Copyright © 2018 Pamela Li.

delinquency, psychopathology and substance abuse (Wang, 2014).

But emotional regulation is not something that we are born with.

Children learn this essential skill through observing, mimicking and practicing.

Terrible-twos is the earliest and most important opportunity to gain this skill.

It is also the time when children should start practicing to eventually attain optimal proficiency.

So, terrible-twos is not just a phase. It is a pivotal time and the results can be life changing.

Copyright © 2018 Pamela Li.

Chapter 8
When To Seek Help?

Tantrums usually begin in children at 12-18 months and stop at around the age of 4.

The American Academy of Pediatrics recommends that you call your pediatrician or family physician if:

- Tantrums get worse after age 4

- Your child's tantrums seem overly frequent or intense

- Your child injures himself or herself or others, or destroys property during tantrums

- Your child holds his or her breath during tantrums, especially if he or she faints

- Your child also has nightmares, reversal of toilet training, headaches, stomachaches, anxiety, refuses to eat or go to bed, or clings to you

Review with the pediatrician your child's developmental and behavioral milestones at routine well-child checkups.

These visits are good opportunities to discuss any concerns you have about your child's behavior, and they help to rule out any serious psychological or physiological problems.

Copyright © 2018 Pamela Li.

Chapter 9
My Toddler's Tantrums

Our daughter was not an easy baby.

Her terrible-twos started when she was only one. The tantrums were so bad that I started researching and blogging about parenting because of that.

It was a very stressful time.

The parenting strategies discussed here are not easy to do. When I first tried them, it seemed like nothing would ever change.

Tantrums continued. My frustration went on.

I almost gave up after many tries.

I had to time-out myself when I felt that I was about to explode.

Sometimes, I was so upset that I couldn't even tell her I was leaving the room to cool off. I just left without saying a word for fear of saying something that I might regret.

Copyright © 2018 Pamela Li.

It took practice for me to remember to put things into perspective.

Over time, I started seeing changes, changes for the better.

I saw changes in her behavior and her personality.

I also felt the changes in my mood and my ability to stay calm.

Those were good lessons for me, too. I learn to regulate my own emotions!

I began to feel the triumph.

Some parents may be worried that this child-centric approach is too lenient. They fear that they will spoil their child and end up raising a monster running the household.

But decades of studies have consistently shown that being nurturing and supportive result in better achieved and more well-adjusted kids.

Being nurturing and supportive is not the same as being permissive or undisciplined. In our house, we still set limits and hold our boundaries.

Copyright © 2018 Pamela Li.

We just do it in a *kind and firm way*.

Not only has our child not turned into a defiant creature, but she has also become one of the most well-behaved kids.

We never worry about her having a meltdown in the toy store or the restaurant.

Of course, she still has her moments and there are always new challenges as she grows, but she is as well behaved as a young child can reasonably be.

After all, her brain, especially the thinking brain part, will not be complete until she is in her mid-twenties.

I learn to be patient!

Our daughter is the happiest and most resilient child I've ever met.

Her swimming coach said that her smile seemed to be permanently stuck on her face because she smiled all the time.

Really, it's ALL the time!

Copyright © 2018 Pamela Li.

The coach had to keep reminding her not to smile while swimming or she would keep choking on the pool water.

We have an excellent relationship.

There is no yelling in our home, only outbursts of laughter.

We couldn't have asked for a better outcome. It was worth the hard work.

I know our job is not done. There will always be new challenges at every stage of her life. I will keep researching, trying and writing about the latest studies in brain science and parenting.

I hope to share more with you in this journey.

Copyright © 2018 Pamela Li.

Thank you for reading!

I hope this eBook has been helpful for you.

For more parenting tips and tricks, join us on Facebook
https://www.facebook.com/parentingforbrai n/

I also invite you to share your thoughts and reviews on Amazon.

Your feedback will help me write better books!

Copyright © 2018 Pamela Li.

Copyright © 2018 Pamela Li.

Author

Pamela is a mother and a bestselling author. Her research-based parenting strategies are highly effective and backed by science. She helps parents create healthy and happy homes that allow children to develop their brains optimally and reach their full potentials. She also helps parents who've had traumatic childhood break the cycle and do it differently with their own children.

The creator and author of popular blog, ParentingForBrain.com, Pamela's named Top Writer on Quora.com answering parenting questions. Her advice has also appeared on HuffPost, HuffPostUK, Apple News and Fatherly.

Pamela is a McGill & Stanford-trained electrical engineer and has received master's degrees from Stanford University and Harvard University.

Copyright © 2018 Pamela Li.

References

Aamodt, S. & Wang, S., 2011. *Welcome To Your Child's Brain. By Sandra Aamodt and Sam Wang.*. s.l.:s.n.

Arnsten, A. F. T., 2009. Stress signalling pathways that impair prefrontal cortex structure and function. *Nature Reviews Neuroscience,* pp. 410-422.

Bakermans-Kranenburg, M. J. & Ijzendoorn, M. H. v., 2011. Differential susceptibility to rearing environment depending on dopamine-related genes: New evidence and a meta-analysis. *Development and Psychopathology / Volume 23 / Issue 01,* pp. 39-52.

Bath, H., 2006. Wiring Pathways to Replace Aggression. *Reclaiming Children and Youth: The Journal of Strength-based Interventions, v14 n4,* pp. 249-251.

Bremner, J., 1999. Does stress damage the brain?. *Biological psychiatry. 45(7),* pp. 797-805.

Bugental, D. B., Martorell, G. A. & Barraza, V., 2003. The hormonal costs of subtle forms of infant maltreatment. *Hormones and Behavior. Volume 43, Issue 1,* p. 237–244.

Carrion, V. G., Weems, C. F. & Reiss, A. L., 2007. Stress Predicts Brain Changes in Children: A Pilot Longitudinal Study on Youth Stress, Posttraumatic Stress Disorder, and the Hippocampus. *PEDIATRICS Vol. 119 No. 3,* pp. 509 -516.

Caspi, A. et al., 2008. Temperamental Origins of Child and Adolescent Behavior Problems: From Age Three to Age Fifteen. *Child Development, Volume 66, Issue 1,* pp. 55-68.

Contreras, J. M. et al., 2000. Emotion regulation as a mediator of associations between mother–child attachment and peer relationships in middle childhood.. *Journal of Family Psychology, Vol 14(1),* pp. 111-124.

Denham, S. et al., 2000. Prediction of externalizing behavior problems from early to middle childhood: The role of parental socialization and emotion expression. *Development and Psychopathology,* pp. 23-45.

Dutra, L. et al., 2009. Quality of Early Care and Childhood Trauma: A Prospective Study of Developmental Pathways to Dissociation. *J Nerv Ment Dis.*

Eisenberger, N., 2012. *The neural bases of social pain: evidence for shared representations with physical pain.*, Los Angeles: University of California, Los Angeles.

Eisenberger, N. I., 2012. The pain of social disconnection: examining the shared neural underpinnings of physical and social pain. *Nature Reviews Neuroscience 13,* pp. 421-434.

Eisenberg, N. et al., 2003. The Relations of Regulation and Emotionality to Children's Externalizing and Internalizing Problem Behavior. *Child Development.*

Eisenberg, N. & Fabes, R. A., 1992. Emotion, regulation, and the development of social competence.. *Social psychology, Vol. 14,* pp. 119-150.

Eisenberg, N., Fabes, R. A. & Murphy, B. C., 1996. Parents' Reactions to Children's Negative.

Eisenberg, N., Fabes, R. A. & Murphy, B. C., 1996. Parents' Reactions to Children's Negative Emotions: Relations to Children's Social

Competence and Comforting Behavior. *Child Development, Volume 67, Issue 5,* p. 2227–2247.

Ervin-Tripp, S., 2014. *Child Discourse.* s.l.:s.n.

Fabes, R. A., Leonard, S. A., Kupanoff, K. & Martin, C. L., 2001. Parental Coping with Children's Negative Emotions: Relations with Children's Emotional and Social Responding. *Child Development, Volume 72, Issue 3,* p. 907–920.

Fabes, R., Leonard, S., Kupanoff, K. & Martin, C., 2001. Parental coping with children's negative emotions: relations with children's emotional and social responding.. *Child development,* pp. 907-20.

Farrant, K. & Reese, E., 2000. Maternal Style and Children's Participation in Reminiscing: Stepping Stones in Children's Autobiographical Memory Development. *Journal of Cognition and Development. Volume 1, Issue 2,* pp. 193-225.

Feehan, M., McGee, R., Stanton, W. & Silva, P., 1991. Strict and inconsistent discipline in childhood: consequences for adolescent mental health.. *The British Journal of Clinical Psychology / the British Psychological Society,* pp. 325-31.

Fivush, R., Marin, K., McWilliams, K. & Bohanek, J. G., 2009. Family Reminiscing Style: Parent Gender and Emotional Focus in Relation to Child Well-Being. *JOURNAL OF COGNITION AND DEVELOPMENT, 10(3),* p. 210–235.

Gadzella, B. M., Ginther, D. W. & Bryant, G. W., 1997. PREDICTION OF PERFORMANCE IN AN ACADEMIC COURSE BY SCORES ON MEASURES OF LEARNING STYLE AND CRITICAL THINKING. *Psychologic Reports. Volume 81,* pp. 595-602.

Gershoff, E. T., 2002. Corporal Punishment by Parents and Associated Child Behaviors and Experiences: A Meta-Analytic and Theoretical Review. *Psychological Bulletin. Vol. 128, No. 4,* p. 539–579.

Gokhale, A. A., 1995. Collaborative Learning Enhances Critical Thinking. *Journal of Technology Education. Volume 7, Number 1.*

Graziano, P. A., Reavis, R. D., Keane, S. P. & Calkins, S. D., 2007. The role of emotion regulation in children's early academic success. *Journal of School Psychology, Volume 45, Issue 1,* p. 3–19.

Hastings, P. D. & Grusec, J. E., 1998. Parenting goals as organizers of responses to parent–child disagreement.. *Developmental Psychology, Vol 34(3),* pp. 465-479.

Heinrichsa, M., Baumgartnera, T., Kirschbaumb, C. & Ehlert, U., 2003. Social support and oxytocin interact to suppress cortisol and subjective responses to psychosocial stress. *Biological Psychiatry, Volume 54, Issue 12,* p. 1389–1398.

Hendriks, M. C., Nelson, J. K., Cornelius, R. R. & Vingerhoets, A. J., 2008. Why Crying Improves Our Well-being: An Attachment-Theory Perspective on the Functions of Adult Crying. *Emotion Regulation,* pp. 87-96.

Holmgren, B. R. & Covin, T. M., 1984. Selective characteristics of preservice professionals.. *Education, Vol 104(3),* pp. 321-328.

Huttenlocher, P. R., 1984. Synapse elimination and plasticity in developing human cerebral cortex.. *American Journal of Mental Deficiency, Vol 88(5),* pp. 488-496.

Izard, C. et al., 2001. Emotion Knowledge as a Predictor of Social Behavior and Academic

Copyright © 2018 Pamela Li.

Competence in Children at Risk. *Psychological Science, vol. 12 no. 1,* pp. 18-23.

Jones, S., Eisenberg, N., Fabes, R. A. & MacKinnon, D. P., 2002. Parents' Reactions to Elementary School Children's Negative Emotions: Relations to Social and Emotional Functioning at School. *Merrill-Palmer Quarterly, Volume 48, Number 2,* pp. 133-159.

Karp, H., 2008. *The Happiest Toddler on the Block: How to Eliminate Tantrums and Raise a Patient, Respectful and Cooperative.* s.l.:s.n.

Keane, S. & Calkins, S., 2004. Predicting kindergarten peer social status from toddler and preschool problem behavior.. *Journal of abnormal child psychology,* pp. 32(4):409-23.

Krug, E. G. et al., 2002. *World report on violence and health,* Geneva: World Health Organization.

Liliana, B. & Nicoleta, T. M., 2014. Personality, Family Correlates and Emotion Regulation as Wellbeing Predictors. *Procedia - Social and Behavioral Sciences, Volume 159,* p. 142–146.

Lopes, P. N., Salovey, P. & Straus, R., 2003. Emotional intelligence, personality, and the

Copyright © 2018 Pamela Li.

perceived quality of social relationships. *Personality and Individual Differences, Volume 35, Issue 3,* p. 641–658.

Luebbe, A. M., Kiel, E. J. & Buss, K. A., 2011. Toddlers' context-varying emotions, maternal responses to emotions, and internalizing behaviors.. *Emotion, Vol 11(3),* pp. 697-703.

Lunkenheimer, E. S., Shields, A. M. & Cortina, K. S., 2007. Parental Emotion Coaching and Dismissing in Family Interaction. *Social Development, Volume 16, Issue 2,* p. 232–248.

Marin, K. A., Bohanek, J. G. & Fivush, R., 2008. Positive Effects of Talking About the Negative: Family Narratives of Negative Experiences and Preadolescents' Perceived Competence. *Journal of Research on Adolescence. Volume 18, Issue 3,* p. 573–593.

Mayseless, O., Scharf, M. & Sholt, M., 2003. From Authoritative Parenting Practices to an Authoritarian Context: Exploring the Person–Environment Fit. *Journal of Research on Adolescence, Volume 13, Issue 4,* p. 427–456.

Copyright © 2018 Pamela Li.

McGill University, n.d. *The Two Pathways Of Fear.*
[Online]
Available at:
http://thebrain.mcgill.ca/flash/d/d_04/d_04_cr
/d_04_cr_peu/d_04_cr_peu.html#2

Mikulincer, M., Shaver, P. R. & Pereg, D., 2003.
Attachment Theory and Affect Regulation: The
Dynamics, Development, and Cognitive
Consequences of Attachment-Related Strategies.
Motivation and Emotion, Volume 27, Issue 2, pp. 77-
102.

Morris, A. S. et al., 2007. The Role of the Family
Context in the Development of Emotion
Regulation. *Social Development, Vol 16 Issue 2,* pp.
361-388.

Polderman, T. J. C. et al., 2015. Meta-analysis of
the heritability of human traits based on fifty years
of twin studies. *Nature Genetics.*

Potegal, M. & Davidson, R., 2003. *Temper Tantrums
in Young Children: 1. Behavioral Composition,*
Madison: University of Wisconsin.

Potegal, M., Kosorok, M. & Davidson, R., 2003.
Temper tantrums in young children: 2. Tantrum duration

Copyright © 2018 Pamela Li.

and temporal organization., Madison: University of Wisconsin.

Potegal, M., Kosorok, M. R. & Davidson, R. J., 2003. Temper Tantrums in Young Children: 2. Tantrum Duration and Temporal Organization. *Journal of Developmental & Behavioral Pediatrics: Volume 24 - Issue 3,* p. 148–154.

Roben, C. K. P., Cole, P. M. & Armstrong, L. M., 2013. Longitudinal Relations Among Language Skills, Anger Expression, and Regulatory Strategies in Early Childhood. *Child Development. Volume 84, Issue 3,* p. 891–905.

Sapolsky, R., Uno, H., Rebert, C. & Finch, C., 1990. Hippocampal damage associated with prolonged glucocorticoid exposure in primates.. *The Journal of Neuroscience. 10(9),* pp. 2897-902.

Seaward, B. L., 2011. *Managing Stress: Principles and Strategies for Health and Wellbeing.* s.l.:s.n.

Stien, P. & Kendall, J. C., 2014. *Psychological Trauma and the Developing Brain: Neurologically Based Interventions for Troubled Children.* s.l.:s.n.

Straus, M. A., 2001. New evidence for the benefits of never spanking. *Society. Volume 38, Issue 6,* pp. 52-60.

Sulzer, D. & Galli, A., 2003. Dopamine transport currents are promoted from curiosity to physiology.. *Trends in neurosciences,* pp. 173-6.

Sunderland, M., 2006. *The Science of Parenting.* New York: DK Publishing Inc.

Thoits, P., 1995. Stress, coping, and social support processes: where are we? What next?. *Journal of health and social behavior,* pp. 53-79.

Tomoda, A. et al., 2009. Reduced prefrontal cortical gray matter volume in young adults exposed to harsh corporal punishment. *NeuroImage. Volume 47, Supplement 2,* p. T66–T71.

Uchino, B. N., Cacioppo, J. T. & Kiecolt-Glaser, J. K., 1996. The Relationship Between Social Support and Physiological Processes:A Review With Emphasis on Underlying Mechanisms and Implications for Health. *PsychoLogical Bulletin,* pp. 488-531.

Copyright © 2018 Pamela Li.

Waters, S., West, T. & Mendes, W., 2014. Stress contagion: physiological covariation between mothers and infants.. *Psychological Science.*

Williams, R. L. et al., 2003. Psychological Critical Thinking As a Course Predictor and Outcome Variable. *Teaching of Psychology. Volume 30, Issue 3,* pp. 220-223.

WINSLER, A. et al., 2003. Private speech in preschool children: developmental stability and change, across-task consistency, and relations with classroom behaviour. *Journal of Child Language / Volume 30 / Issue 03,* pp. 583-608.